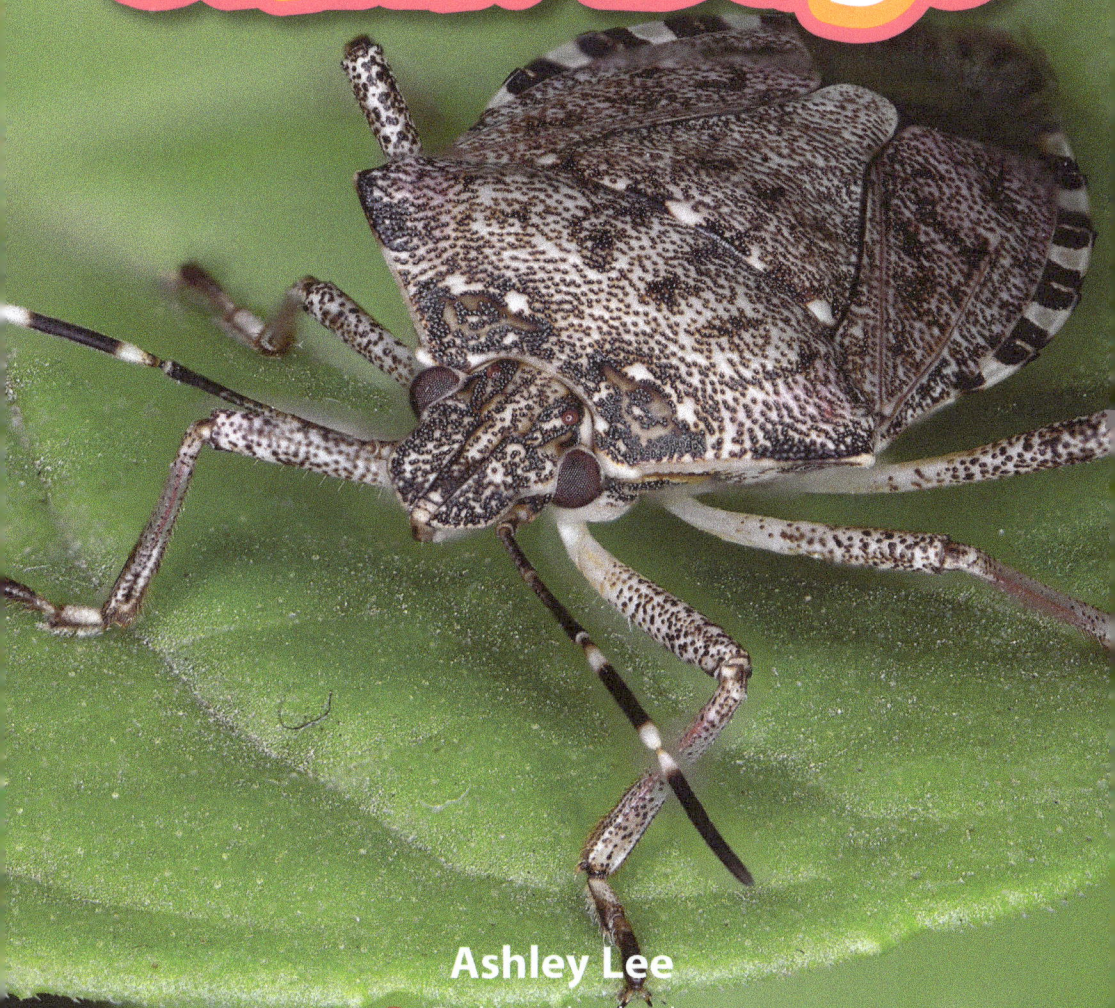

Backyard Bugs & Creepy-Crawlies

Stink Bugs

Ashley Lee

Explore other books at:
WWW.ENGAGEBOOKS.COM

VANCOUVER, B.C.

e WWW.ENGAGEBOOKS.COM

Stink Bugs: Level 1
Backyard Bugs & Creepy Crawlies
Lee, Ashley 1995 –
Text © 2022 Engage Books
Design © 2022 Engage Books

Edited by: A.R. Roumanis

Text set in Epilogue

FIRST EDITION / FIRST PRINTING

LIBRARY AND ARCHIVES CANADA CATALOGUING IN PUBLICATION

Title: Stink Bugs / Ashley Lee.
Names: Lee, Ashley, author.
Description: Series statement: Backyard bugs & creepy-crawlies
Engaging readers: level 1, beginner.

Identifiers: Canadiana (print) 20250448542 | Canadiana (ebook) 20250448569
ISBN 978-1-77878-712-6 (hardcover)
ISBN 978-1-77878-721-8 (softcover)

Subjects:
LCSH: Stink Bugs—Juvenile literature.

Classification: LCC QL737.P94 C38 2025 | DDC J599.885—DC23

This project has been made possible in part by the Government of Canada.

Canada

Contents

What Are Stink Bugs?

Stink bugs are small insects. There are over 4,500 kinds of stink bugs.

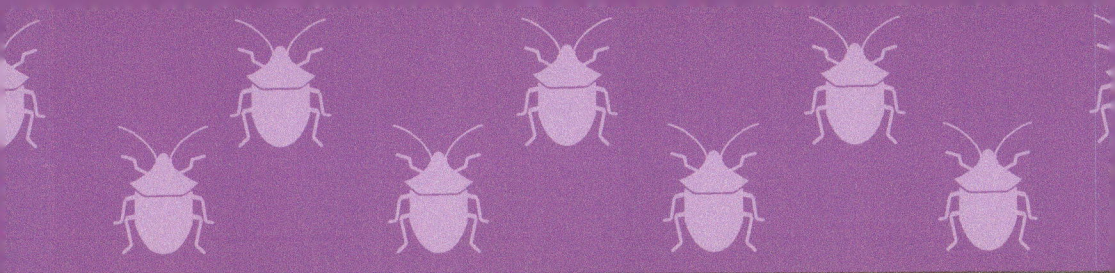

People sometimes call them "**shield** bugs." This is because their bodies are shaped like shields.

Key Word

Shield: a piece of metal someone holds to protect themselves.

5

What Do Stink Bugs Look Like?

Stink bugs are often brown or green. Some have red or yellow markings.

Stink bugs have two long feelers. Each feeler is made up of five pieces.

6

Feelers

7

Adult stink bugs have wings. They fold them on their backs.

Stink bug mouths are shaped like straws. They stick their mouth into food and suck out the juices.

Where Do Stink Bugs Live?

Stink bugs live on most continents. They do not live in Antarctica.

Key Word

Continents: the seven major areas of land on Earth.

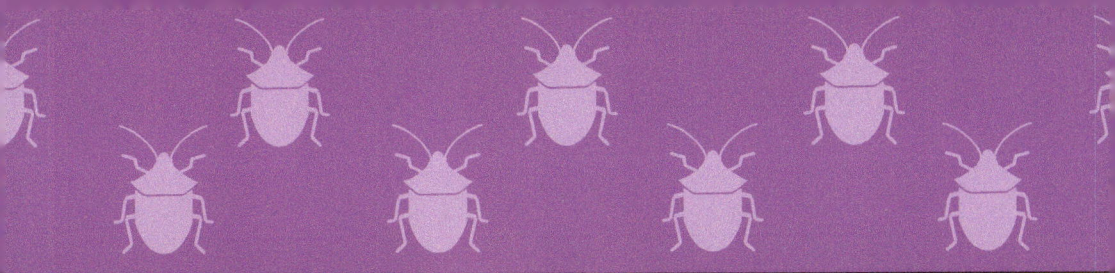

They like to live near farms with lots of food. They are often found on trees and other plants.

What Do Stink Bugs Eat?

Some stink bugs are herbivores. This means they only eat plants.

Different kinds of stink bugs eat different plants. Many stink bugs eat fruit.

Some stink bugs are carnivores. This means they eat meat.

A few stink bugs eat plants when they are young. They switch to eating meat as they get older.

Stink Bug Behavior

Stink bugs sometimes give off a bad smell. They do this when in danger.

Other animals leave stink bugs alone when they smell bad. They do not want to eat smelly food.

17

Stink bugs do not like the cold. They hide in people's houses in winter.

They go into a sleep-like state. This helps them survive the winter.

19

Stink Bug Life Cycle

Female stink bugs lay eggs in spring. They lay eggs on leaves or plant stems.

Eggs are laid in groups called clusters. There are between 5 and 50 eggs in a cluster.

Baby stink bugs are called nymphs. Nymphs shed their skin. This helps them grow.

Stink bugs have short lives. They live for six to eight months.

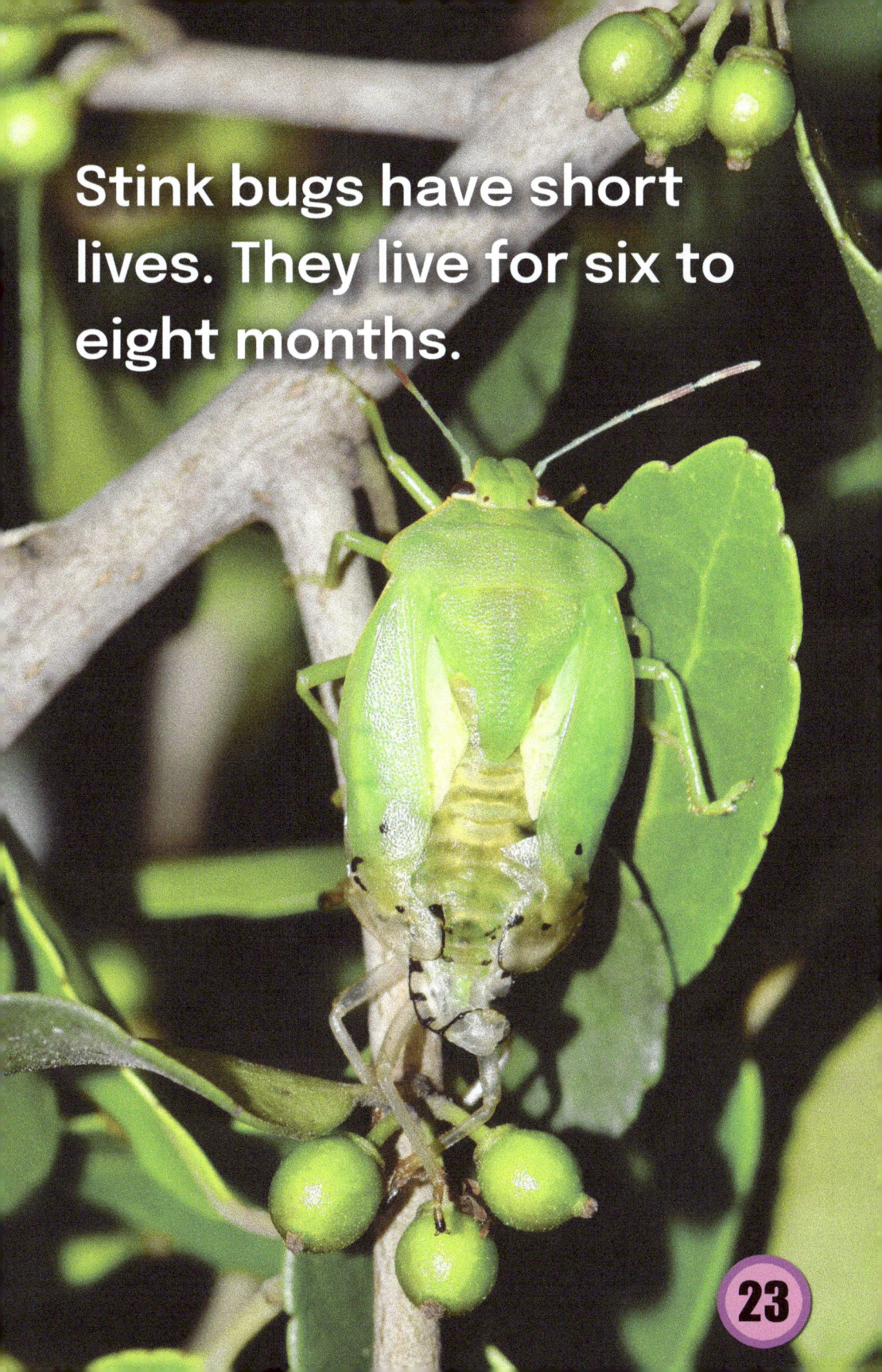

Fun Facts

Some people eat stink bugs.

Stink bugs talk to each other using **vibrations**.

Key Word

Vibrations: fast back and forth movements.

Some people think stink bugs smell like cilantro.

It is hard to get rid of stink bugs once they are in your home.

Are Stink Bugs Helpful or Harmful?

Some stink bugs harm gardens. They eat food being grown for humans.

People do not like when stink bugs eat their food. They spray **pesticides** to get rid of them.

Key Word

Pesticides: something sprayed on plants to get rid of bugs.

27

Are Stink Bugs in Danger?

Stink bugs are not in danger. There are lots of them all over the world.

Some places have too many stink bugs. Too many stink bugs can cause farms to be harmed.

29

Quiz

Test your knowledge of stink bugs by answering the following questions. The questions are based on what you have read in this book. The answers are listed on the bottom of the next page.

1 Are stink bugs small insects?

2 Do adult stink bugs have wings?

3 Do stink bugs live in Antarctica?

4 Do stink bugs like the cold?

5 Do stink bugs have short lives?

6 Do people like when stink bugs eat their food?

Explore other books in the
Backyard Bugs & Creepy Crawlies series!

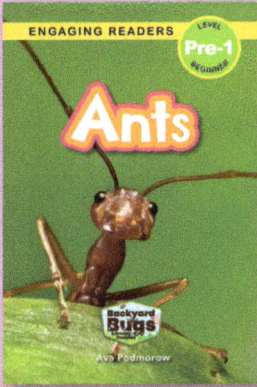

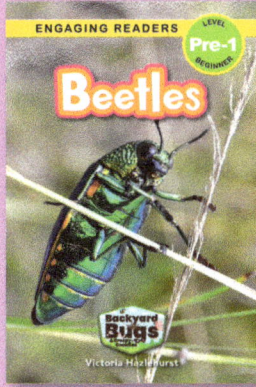

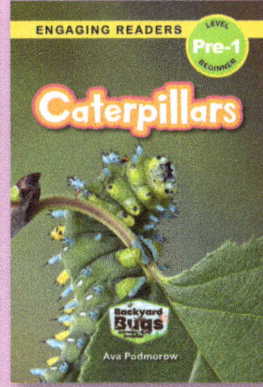

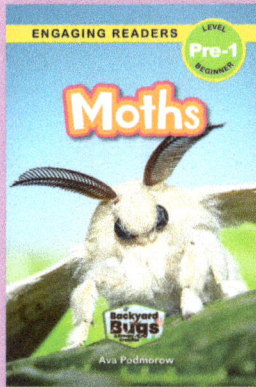

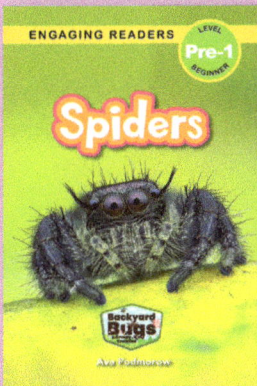

Visit www.engagebooks.com to explore more Engaging Readers.

Answers: 1. Yes 2. Yes 3. No 4. No 5. Yes 6. No

www.ingramcontent.com/pod-product-compliance
Lightning Source LLC
Chambersburg PA
CBHW052037030426
42337CB00027B/5038